A Look at France

by Helen Frost

Consulting Editor: Gail Saunders-Smith, Ph.D.

Consultant: Elizabeth Kiken
Managing Editor, *News from France*
Press and Communication Department
Embassy of France, Washington, D.C.

Pebble Books

an imprint of Capstone Press
Mankato, Minnesota

Pebble Books are published by Capstone Press
151 Good Counsel Drive, P.O. Box 669, Mankato, Minnesota 56002
http://www.capstone-press.com

2 3 4 5 6 07 06 05 04 03 02

Library of Congress Cataloging-in-Publication Data
Frost, Helen, 1949–
    A look at France / by Helen Frost.
    p. cm.—(Our world)
    Includes bibliographical references and index.
    Summary: Introduces the land, animals, and people of France.
    ISBN 0-7368-1167-2 (hardcover)
    ISBN 0-7368-4856-8 (paperback)
    1. France—Juvenile literature. [1. France.] I. Title. II. Our world (Pebble Books)
DC17 .F76 2002
944—dc21   2001003309

Pebble Books thanks the Embassy of France in Washington, D.C., for its help
with this book. The author thanks the children's section staff at Allen County Public
Library in Fort Wayne, Indiana, for research assistance.

Note to Parents and Teachers

The Our World series supports national social studies standards
related to culture. This book describes and illustrates the land,
animals, and people of France. The photographs support early
readers in understanding the text. The repetition of words and
phrases helps early readers learn new words. This book also
introduces early readers to subject-specific vocabulary words, which
are defined in the Words to Know section. Early readers may need
assistance to read some words and to use the Table of Contents,
Words to Know, Read More, Internet Sites, and Index/Word List
sections of the book.

Table of Contents

★ Paris

France

France is one of
the largest countries
in Europe. The capital
of France is Paris.

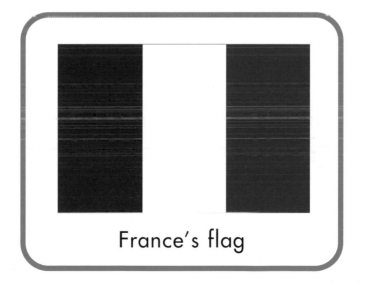

France's flag

mountains

plains

river valley

plateau

6

France has mountains, plains, river valleys, and plateaus. Most of France has mild weather.

lynx

flamingo

8

Lynx live on France's mountains. Flamingos live in southern France.

More than 59 million
people live in France.
Most people live in
Paris and other cities.
French is the country's
official language.

Pétanque is a popular game in France. Many French people also enjoy skiing and tennis.

Many artists, writers, and filmmakers live in France. French chefs are famous for their desserts and sauces.

GV 176164

GV 1
HEDROUZ

French workers catch
and sell fish to earn money.
French workers make
cars, airplanes, and trains.

France's money is
counted in euros.

French people travel by car, airplane, and train. Some trains travel in a tunnel beneath the English Channel.

The Eiffel Tower is
in Paris. Visitors take
an elevator to the top
of the Eiffel Tower.
They look at the
city lights at night.

Words to Know

capital—the city where a country's government is based; the capital of France is Paris.

Eiffel Tower—a tall tower in Paris; the Eiffel Tower was built in 1889; it is 984 feet (300 meters) high; Gustave Eiffel designed the Eiffel Tower.

English Channel—a narrow part of the Atlantic Ocean that flows between France and England; a tunnel for trains and cars was built under the English Channel in 1994.

language—the words and grammar that people use to talk and write to each other

Paris—the capital city of France; one-sixth of the people in France live in Paris.

pétanque (pay-TAHK)—a French game played with small metal balls; pétanque is similar to bowling; it is popular in the south of France; pétanque also is called boules.

plateau—an area of high, flat land

Read More

Alcraft, Rob. *A Visit to France.* Des Plaines, Ill.: Heinemann Library, 1999.

Boast, Clare. *France.* Next Stop! Des Plaines, Ill.: Heinemann Library, 1998.

Conboy, Fiona, and Roseline NgCheong-Lum. *Welcome to France.* Welcome to My Country. Milwaukee: Gareth Stevens, 2000.

Landau, Elaine. *France.* A True Book. Danbury, Conn.: Children's Press, 2000.

Internet Sites

Embassy of France: Just for Kids
http://www.ambafrance-us.org/kids

France Geography
http://www.photius.com/wfb2000/countries/france/france_geography.html

On the Line—Virtual Journey of France
http://www.ontheline.org.uk/explore/journey/france/frindex.htm

Index/Word List

Word Count: 152
Early-Intervention Level: 16

Editorial Credits
Mari C. Schuh, editor; Kia Bielke, cover designer; Jennifer Schonborn, production designer and illustrator; Kimberly Danger and Jo Miller, photo researchers

Photo Credits
Alison M. Jones, All Rights Reserved, 6 (lower left), 8 (bottom), 12
Arthur Tilley/FPG International LLC, cover
Corel Corporation, 8 (top)
Daniel Grogan/Pictor, 6 (upper left)
Dave G. Houser/Housestock, 14
Digital Stock, 1, 20
J. C. Carton/Bruce Coleman Inc., 17 (bill)
John Elk III, 6 (lower right), 16, 18
One Mile Up, Inc., 5
Pictor, 10
Reuters/HO/Archive Photos, 17 (coin)
Victor Englebert, 6 (upper right)